Failure Is Not The END

It Is An Emotional Gym

Complete Workout Plan On How To Build Your Emotional Muscle And Burning Down Anxiety To Become Emotionally Stronger, More Confident and Less Reactive

Your Free Gift

As a way of thanking you for the purchase, I'd like to offer you a complimentary gift:

- **5 Pillar Life Transformation Checklist:** This short book is about life transformation, presented in bit size pieces for easy implementation. I believe that without such a checklist, you are likely to have a hard time implementing anything in this book and any other thing you set out to do religiously and sticking to it for the long haul. It doesn't matter whether your goals relate to weight loss, relationships, personal finance, investing, personal development, improving communication in your family, your overall health, finances, improving your sex life, resolving issues in your relationship, fighting PMS successfully, investing, running a successful business, traveling etc. With a checklist like this one, you can bet that anything you do will seem a lot easier to implement until the end. Therefore, even if you don't continue reading this book, at least read the one thing that will help you in every other aspect of your life. Grab your copy now by clicking/tapping here or simply enter http://bit.ly/2fantonfreebie into your browser. Your life will never be the same again (if you implement what's in this book), I promise.

PS: I'd like your feedback. If you are happy with this book, please leave a review on Amazon.

Introduction

'When we understand the privilege of what it means to be an athlete, we are in touch with and rejoice in, our physical, mental and emotional strengths and our endless possibilities.'- Gloria Averbuch

While we label only the people participating in some sport or physical activity as athletes, the truth is all of us are athletes in our own right. Every day, we have many challenges to fight, many obstacles to overcome and many struggles to win over. During this process, we need to make sure we stay put, maintain our calm and confidence and take care of our emotional and mental well-being so that we don't stumble every now and then, stay strong and survive the hardships that come along our way.

As much as it is important to take care of your physical health and workout to ensure you stay strong in the face of adversity, it is equally, in fact even more substantial to pay attention to your emotional and mental health. You need to exercise your emotional muscle and work out your mind as much as you need to work out your body in order for it to stay alert, sharp, mindful, focused and strong to help you strive for better and achieve your goals.

Your brain is a muscle that needs exercise as much as all the other muscles in your body do to stay fit and flexible, and if you aren't working out your emotional muscle effectively, it is likely your mental wellbeing will deteriorate with time. You sure don't want that to happen to you right. In that case, just keep reading along because this book equips you with the knowledge and guidance to better take care of your emotional and mental health and provides you with an actionable and potent workout for your brain to ensure it stays active, focused and confident.

Table of Contents

Chapter 1: Understanding Emotional Muscle And The Importance Of Working It Out

There are around 650 to 840 muscles in the human body and while physicians and health experts often talk about the importance of exercising the different muscles especially those pertinent to your limbs and abdomen, often there is one muscle that does not come in the limelight as much as it is supposed to. If you haven't guessed already, I am referring to your emotional muscle.

Let us start with the basics and begin with having a clearer understanding of what emotional muscle is and then detailing out the importance of exercising it.

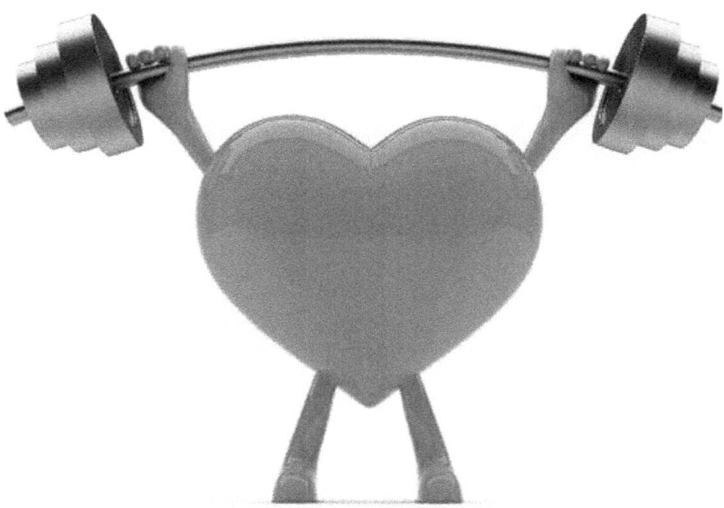

Definition of Emotional Muscle and Emotional Intelligence

To better understand emotional muscle and your ability to exercise it, you first need to have an understanding of emotional intelligence. Mostly, people think that IQ is the determinant of one's success. However, experts and studies have now validated that emotional intelligence (EI) is the real factor at play determining your success in any and every aspect of life.

Emotional intelligence refers to your ability to be aware of your emotions as well as those of other people around you and manage both, your emotions and those of others successfully. In his book, 'Emotional Intelligence: Why it Can Matter More Than IQ, Daniel Goleman highlighted the 5 major components of EI:

- Self-awareness: This refers to your ability to be aware of emotions and what drives them. Oftentimes, we aren't aware of how and what we feel, but it is when we become more conscious of the different emotions we experience and the underlying feelings that induce them, can we find effective ways to manage them.

- Internal Motivation: This refers to your passion to work towards a certain goal. You need to be internally motivated to do something to ensure you work committedly towards a goal and actualize it. To be motivated, you need to be aware of your emotions that drive your motivation.

- Self-regulation: This refers to your ability to rationally think before taking any action and to redirect different disruptive moods and impulses. Often, when you experience an unfortunate situation, you react to it, which usually encompasses an irrational decision on your part. For instance, if you have an argument with your partner, you are likely to react by saying mean things to him/ her. However, when you have the ability to regulate your emotions, you are able to control your urge to react to things and think things through to respond to situations instead of reacting to them. When you respond and not react to things, you are likely to take informed decisions and stay calm to better use your emotions.

- Empathy: It refers to understanding the emotions and feelings of others and feeling them as your own. It is only when you can actually feel the pain and joy of others that you take effective actions to manage different situations appropriately.

- Social Skills: This refers to the ability to effectively build rapport with people and maintain relationships successfully.

To succeed in life and achieve excellence in different aspects of your life including health, career, relationships, happiness, spirituality and emotional wellbeing, you need to have all of the 5 elements of emotional intelligence. This is possible when you have mental strength, which is the ability to stay strong in the face of adversity and manage your emotions to use them effectively. To be mentally strong and resilient, you need to exercise your emotional muscle.

It is by exercising your emotional muscle that you make it bigger, stronger and more powerful and are then able to increase your emotional intelligence. Emotional muscle basically refers to your mind and emotions and it is only by building your mind's strength and gaining emotional resilience that you can build and increase your emotional intelligence.

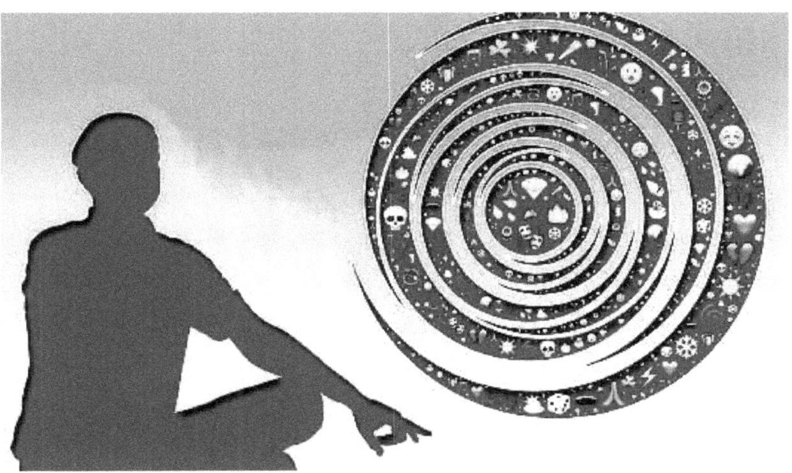

Let us understand better how training your emotional muscle helps you do that by getting insight into some body muscle and emotional muscle training analogies.

Chapter 2: Body Muscle And Emotional Muscle Training Analogies

Colloquially, emotional muscle is your willpower, which is incredibly similar to body muscles. Both grow stronger, bigger and sturdier with training and exercise. Let us dig deeper into the similarities the two share in this chapter and get a clearer understanding of how training your emotional muscle gives you the power to take charge of your life.

How Emotional and Body Muscles Function in a Similar Manner

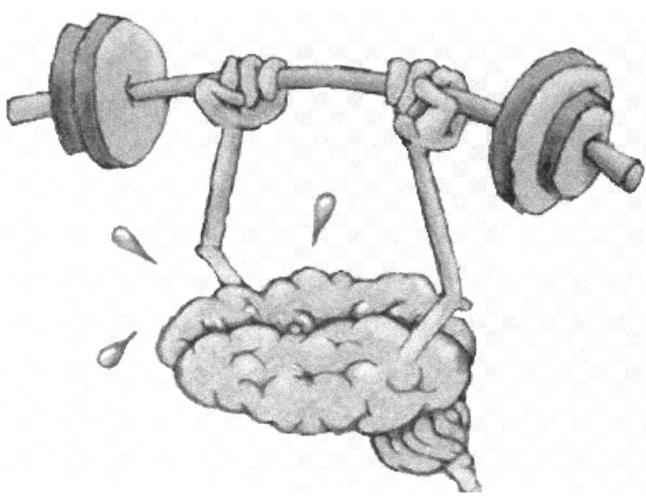

How do you think a bodybuilder inculcates in himself/ herself the ability to lift heavier weights? Of course, by exercising and training himself to lift heavy weights. Exercise and strength training strengthens his muscles and builds in them the power to work harder and become robust enough to bear the load of huge weights. You cannot expect someone with weak muscles or someone who does not train as hard to lift the same amount of load. That is because his/ her muscles would not be tough enough to bear that load.

Strong Emotional Muscle Helps You Fight Emotional Pressures

Just as you need a brawny body to be able to bear physical pressure and load, you need mental strength to withstand the pressure of different obstacles, challenges and traumatic life episodes to power through them and stick to what you believe in.

If you are emotionally weak, you are quite likely to succumb to different pressures and challenges that you encounter in life. You may not be able to handle a financial crisis that well and may succumb to depression; or you may lose heart when your partner leaves you and may never find the courage to have another intimate relationship with someone else in life.

As opposed to this, if you are emotionally strong and resilient, you do become upset, frustrated and even depressed during tough times but you make sure not to give up even in the most challenging times. You power through, get back up and move on like a soldier marching gracefully in war, every time life throws an obstacle your way. Therefore, you may feel your entire world is crashing up on you, but you will still stand up and fight it like a warrior.

You need to be mentally and emotionally powerful, resilient and gritty to tackle the many experiences in life that can easily drive you insane. You cannot expect to stay put and look after your kids when you have just witnessed the death of their father; or you cannot muster the courage and strength to look for ways to earn an income and pay all your debt to become financially stable when you have just lost your job, if your emotional muscle is weak.

If you are robust physically, you can bear the weight of physical pressures. Similarly, if you are emotionally robust, you can withstand every pressure that takes a toll on your mind and your ability to tackle emotional pressures. This is what separates those who give in to pressures from those who do not just complain of what is missing from their life and actually achieve their goals.

If you are aware of Thomas Edison's story, you would know that he tried over 900 attempts to create a successful invention, but every attempt he did, ended in failure. However, that did not stop him from trying his hand at another invention. He kept trying to work things out in his favor and finally on his thousandth attempt, he created the light bulb that actually worked and turned out to be his golden ticket to success.

Edison did not have any magical elixir or a wand that helped him become successful. He did have an amazing power, which turned out to be the magical potion that took him to success. He was mentally strong and he knew how to constantly strengthen and train his emotional muscle so he never gave in to any setback that he experienced and kept moving forward successfully. You too need this very ability to ensure you never settle in for any less than what you know you deserve and always actualize your goals.

Emotional Strength is Acquired by Pushing Yourself Harder

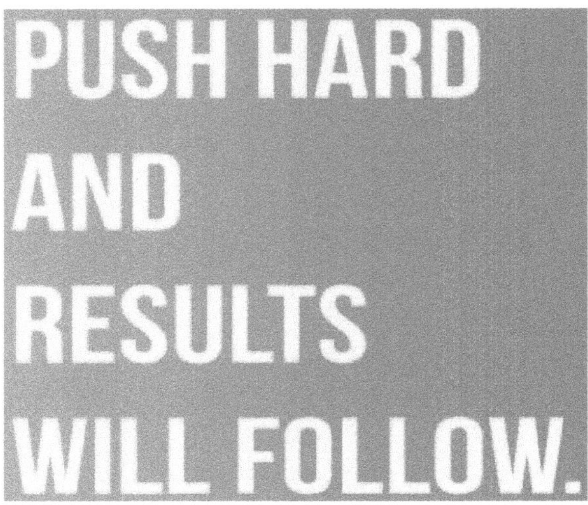

You gain physical strength by pushing yourself harder and by forcing yourself to exercise even when you don't want to. For instance, you may be tempted to just sleep for another hour instead of hitting the gym; or you may feel like only munching on crisps instead of eating salad; however, you are well aware of the consequences of surrendering to your temptations and since you know doing that would get in the way of your goals so you choose training harder over your temptations. Hence, by pushing yourself harder every time in every aspect of training, you are able to build brawnier muscles and physical strength that enables you to achieve all your fitness-elated goals.

Similarly, it is when you constantly exercise your emotional muscle that you are able to gain the emotional strength;

intelligence and grit that helps you battle every obstacle in life and emerge victorious in the end. If you just find out that you have been handed a huge presentation and you have to hand it over in a day, which seems impossible to you, you are quite likely not to meet the deadline and just wallow over your misery if you are mentally weak. You won't tackle that pressure because you won't have the ability to do so. If only you push yourself harder and force yourself to try your hand at that presentation, you will actually be able to complete it on time. You may think of that task as an impossible one, but that is because you are not aware of the power of pushing yourself forward.

The same applies to building body muscle. If you keep lifting the same amount of weights repeatedly, you eventually build the ability to lift them quite easily. Once you are comfortable picking up that amount of weight, it will stop intimidating you and you will actually lift them quite easily. However, your physical strength will then start to stagnate because you will not be pushing yourself anymore.

To keep growing your body muscle, you need to keep pushing your boundaries and increase the load you lift depending on your pace obviously. However, pushing yourself forward is important to achieve more growth. To encourage yourself to go the extra mile, you need to strongly believe in yourself.

Belief Takes You Forward

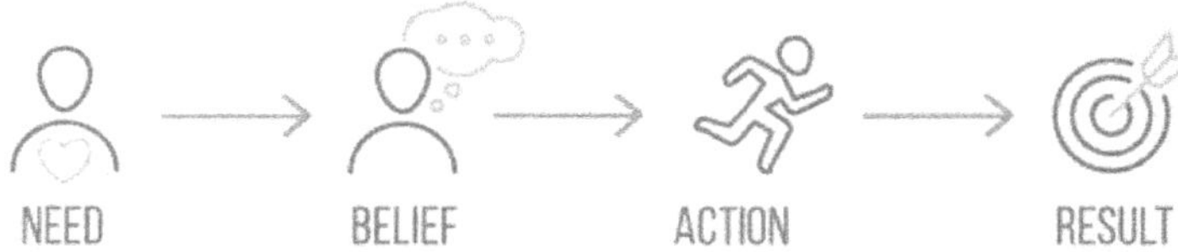

A major reason why you stop pushing yourself forward and accept a setback as your fate is that you believe you do not have what it takes to fight that obstacle. This shows another element of emotional strength- belief. You need to believe that you can do something to be able to push yourself forward towards a certain target and achieve it. If you believe you can do something, you do not let a pressure take over you and your chances to succeed. Instead, you get on your feet and do whatever you can to embrace your goal.

The same applies to physical strength and building body muscle. You need to believe you can do it to actually be able to train harder. Unless you believe you can lift 90kg weights, you will not force yourself to even try picking up that weight. Belief is indeed the most powerful emotion there is.

Resting Helps You Get Better

BETTER SLEEP LEADS TO A BETTER TOMORROW

Another similarity between body muscle and emotional muscle is that a resting period actually helps both these muscles become stronger. When you rest well, you rejuvenate your enthusiasm, motivation, discipline and the desire to work harder. As you feel better to work towards a goal or tackle even the routine hardships of life, you battle them with courage, perseverance, resilience and determination and get all that you aspire for. This is similar to regaining your energy and strengthening your muscle power after a good period of rest. This is why often experts believe in the notion 'failure equals growth.' Let us explore it in detail in the next chapter.

Chapter 3: Muscle Failure Prerequisite To Growth

'Failure is an absolute pre=requisite to success. You learn to succeed from failing.'- Brian Tracy

While many of us fear failing at a task and deem a failure or two as the validation of our incompetency, the truth is far from that. The setbacks you encounter on your way to a goal even a couple of failures are in no way a testament of your weakness or inability to perform well at something. They are in fact the obstacles that aim to shape you into a better and more confident individual because every setback that you encounter gives insight into your weaknesses and shortcomings, which if you improve on can help you become a refined version of yourself.

To succeed in life, you need to be strong enough to take failures and handle them with grace.

Failure Takes You Forward Towards Growth

What would you do if you weren't afraid?

Unfortunately, the term 'failure' has gained quite a bad rap over the years. It is often seen as an unfortunate experience that proves that you can no longer move forward in life. Some people also go as far as perceiving it as a death sentence. Sadly, this attitude only keeps you from achieving your goals because once you strongly believe that you have failed at something, you are quite likely never to try your hand at it again.

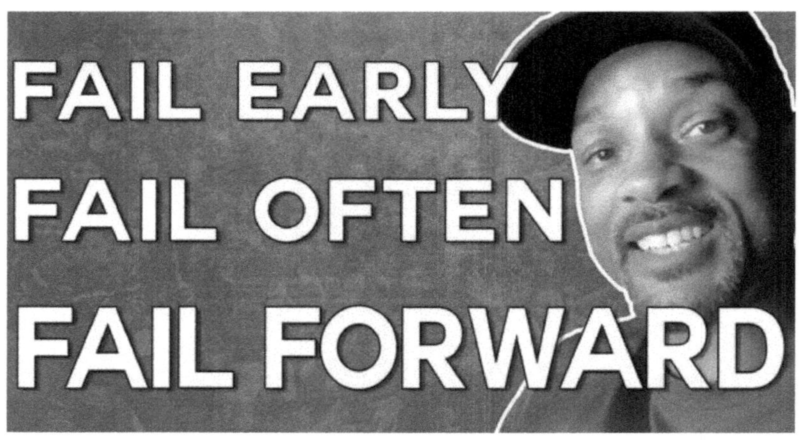

This isn't just true for building a can-do mindset, but also for building your physical strength. Muscle failure is referred to as the point at which you can no longer carry out any more repetitions primarily because you have exhausted your ability to repeat the same reps again and are now in need of some rest. It is after a nice resting period that you regain the ability to train harder and then even push yourself harder to work out even better.

Therefore, when your muscles become exhausted and you feel you cannot go forth with the same routine again, you may feel that you have reached stagnancy and that your muscles have failed at working harder, but that is not a sign of your incompetency. That failure is just a tiny glitch that you need to overcome with investing more effort, perseverance and rest.

Yes, you need to spend some time resting and relaxing to improve your chances of winning. An athlete who cannot compete at a competition because he has incurred a foot injury hasn't failed at proving his talent, worth and might to the world. Instead, he just needs some time to rest and rejuvenate his energy. Rest not only relaxes his muscles and helps heal his internal wounds, but it also helps him recover emotionally and enable him to regain the zeal, zest and motivation he needs to muster up courage to achieve his target again.

Research shows that exercising requires the same strength and cognitive effort as well. Your brain requires more glucose from your blood when you need to exercise greater willpower to work harder. When your willpower depletes, you need more glucose in your bloodstream and an unavailability of it leads to exhaustion. You feel you cannot move forward to actualize your goals because you lack the energy and power to move successfully towards your goals. This is the feeling of 'helplessness and hopelessness' that makes you feel that you cannot ever achieve what you aspire for.

This happens also because a setback does exhaust you. When you fail at achieving a certain target, you feel you do not have what it takes to fulfill your goals. This feels demotivating and then depletes your willpower. While you may feel it is your inability to do something, it is actually your body's way of signaling you to take some rest to revitalize your spirits so that you can slowly build up your glucose supply and fuel your motivation. This then reinforces your emotional muscle providing you with the necessary grit to muster the strength to go for another fight to achieve what you truly believe in.

Another important point to highlight here is the development of a can-do attitude. It is indeed a pre-requisite to building your inner confidence to strive for what you believe in, inculcate self-belief and build the awareness to realize your needs, potential and aspirations and work to achieve them. You need to strongly feel that you CAN do something to become unstoppable. This belief is a pre-requisite for strengthening both your emotional and body muscles. It is only when you are sure that you have what it takes to fulfill your commitment that you are ready to take another round of hardships that can intimidate you and debilitate your confidence.

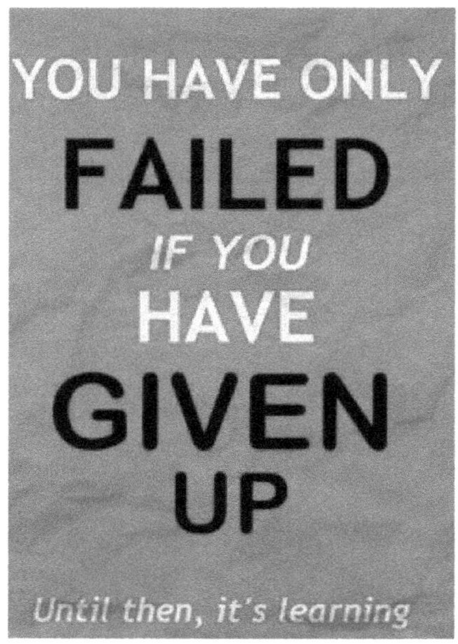

To ensure you build that inner confidence and self-belief, you have to work on assuaging your inner anxiety. Let us talk about it in the next chapter.

Chapter 4: Burning Down Anxiety

To become physically healthier, stronger and sturdier in order to get the right body to perform better or become the swimming champion or the best international boxer or whatever goal you are chasing, you need to burn the extra weight you have put on.

This goal is not a very simple one; you have to follow a strenuous plan to burn calories, lower your cholesterol level and achieve the right amount of body fat to ensure your body has the strength and ability to fight for your goal. Getting in shape does demand a lot of effort from your end and once you are gradually able to lose weight, you do build a nice, muscular body.

The same principle of burning calories applies to building and sustaining your emotional muscle as well. In emotional muscle training, burning calories is replaced with burning anxiety. Let us get better insight into this phenomenon.

Melt Your Inner Anxiety to Build Your Emotional Muscle

Anxiety is the feeling of nervousness, apprehension, jitteriness and unrest mixed with fear and ediginess you experience right before doing something important, challenging, tough or scary. This is rooted in the stress response your body sets off the minute it feels a challenge or life-altering situation is going to befall you. The fear you feel right before taking an exam or the nervousness you go through before asking your crush out on a date is the perfect example of feeling anxious.

While occasional bouts of anxiety in actually scary situations are fine since anxiety prepares you to battle the difficult situation or flee it to save yourself, it is important to make sure that you don't allow it to become a constant in your life.

If you feel anxious all the time, which many of us often experience, you are quite likely to lack the ability to battle obstacles like a warrior. If you feel uneasy, restless and scared to combat the challenges you face in routine life and those pertinent to a particular goal, you will not work towards achieving it.

For instance, if every time you try to work on your goal of overcoming drug abuse or starting your own stationary subscription business, you feel that you will not be able to do it and a strong sense of agitation and fear takes over you, you will keep putting off working on your goal and will never achieve it.

Anxiety is often the reason why you postpone working on your goals. When you feel scared of working on a task because it is too challenging or because you lack the ability to work on it or because you fear failing or because you have not worked on something for a long time, you are likely to put off working on that very task for a long time. If you procrastinate for too long, it turns into a habit, a habit that then starts to interfere with your routine chores, efficiency and prosperity.

Moreover, when anxiety takes over you every time you try to do something, it overrides your ability to think clearly. This makes you succumb to analysis paralysis, which is the inability to take action because you overthink a lot. Overthinking is quite an unhealthy habit because it only increases your anxiety and sabotages your chances of living a happy life.

When you feel anxious before doing something, you are likely to get into the 'ifs' and 'buts' of doing that task and instead of working on a chore right away, you keep assessing the pros and cons of doing it, go over the right technique to work on it a thousand times and obsess over it so much that after some time you just cannot work on that task anymore.

This feeling is true for both, working to build emotional strength as well as muscle strength. It is only by overcoming that unwanted and unpleasant feeling of constant anxiety that you can actually move towards your action plan and do something meaningful for real to achieve a certain goal. If you keep thinking of how you cannot do something, you will doubt yourself and self-doubt only aggravates your problems and never lets you resolve them for real.

When you melt down your inner anxiousness, you feel light and calm within. This calmness lets you think clearly and focus on what is important so you ignore the background noise and do what you know is right for you. As soon as the cloud of anxiety is cleared off your mind, you become mindful of the present and that helps you inculcate in you the power to believe in yourself. When you are no longer scared of the unknown, you start to believe that you can do something and this motivates you to work harder and achieve what you believe is rightfully yours.

Now that you are aware of why you need to burn down anxiety and why it is crucial for you to build your emotional muscle, let us move on to the next chapter where I share with you a work out plan that can help you strength train your mind to build the mental toughness you need to succeed in life.

Chapter 5: A Workout Plan

If you have a strong, brawny emotional muscle, working out in the gym for even hours seems possible. This is because of the can-do attitude that you have built. When you feel ready to take any challenge that comes your way and overcome every possible obstacle that can get in the way of the fulfillment of your goals, you keep pushing yourself forward and become invincible. Therefore, to train your body, you have to train your mind first. Here is an extremely effective workout plan for training your emotional muscle which if you work on consistently can help you attain both, muscle and mental toughness successfully.

Affirm Positive Suggestions to Your Mind

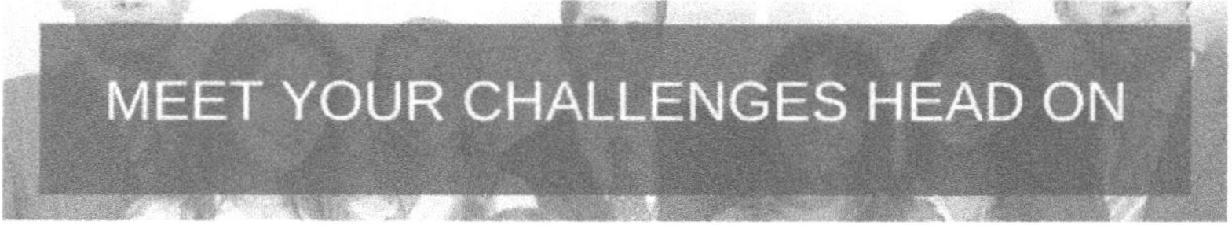

The first exercise of your workout plan is to practice positive affirmations right when you wake up and then 3 to 4 times throughout the day especially before starting an important task.

An affirmation is anything you put your faith in and trust as the truth. When you believe something to be the truth, you focus your mind's energy towards it and become attentive towards it. For instance, if you keep thinking how you cannot work out for an hour today, you will eventually not work out at all that day because you kept giving that very suggestion to your mind the entire day. To train your mind to think positively and become stronger, you need to supply it with positive affirmations so that you rewire it to think positively.

Every morning when you wake up, tell yourself, 'Today is going to be a fantastic day and I will work on all my targets to improve my productivity.' You can obviously create any other positive affirmation you like, just make sure that it is not too long and is purely positive. Chant it confidently, loudly and clearly about 10 times and within minutes, you will start believing in its power. Every time you are supposed to do a difficult or important task, create a positive affirmation based on it and chant it loudly so you focus your subconscious mind on that task and how you can achieve it to eventually embrace it.

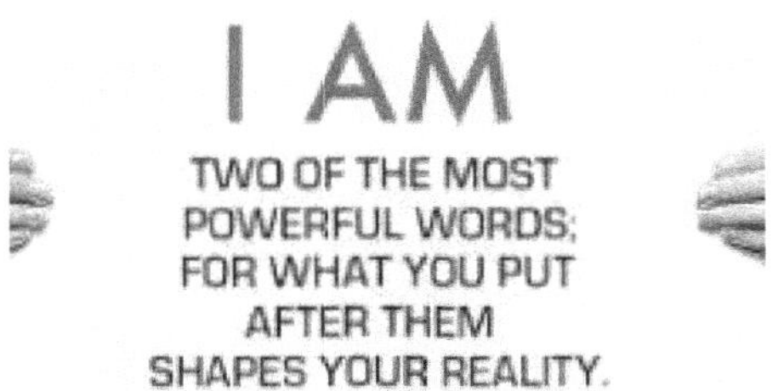

Also, every time you have a negative thought, replace it with a positive affirmation. This way you train yourself to talk positively to yourself at all times and once your self-talk becomes positive, you automatically increase your self-confidence and can easily calm down your nerves when the going gets tough.

Do Something Emotionally Uncomfortable Every Day

As you are already aware of how pushing yourself outside your comfort zone is beneficial to you, slowly nurture the habit of doing at least one emotionally uncomfortable thing every day. When you do something outside your comfort zone or something different, new neuronal pathways are created that strengthens your brainpower and improves your cognitive abilities.

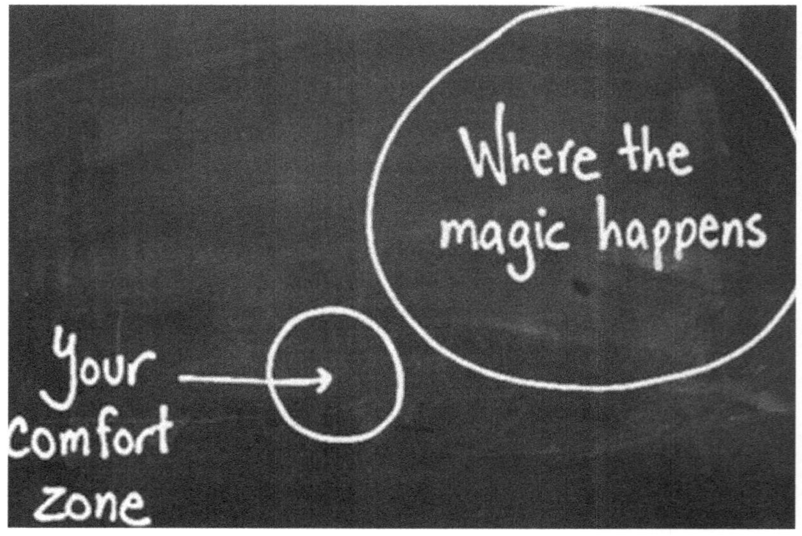

Moreover, doing different and emotionally challenging things makes you try new things, take new risks and learn to adjust to new changes. This improves your emotional strength helping you become grittier with time.

To achieve that, try something emotionally uncomfortable every day of the week. It could be anything from encouraging yourself to talk to a stranger to control your anger when you feel you will just burst to trying an activity that you find boring. This slowly pushes you outside your comfort zone and reinforces your emotional muscle.

Inculcate Mindfulness

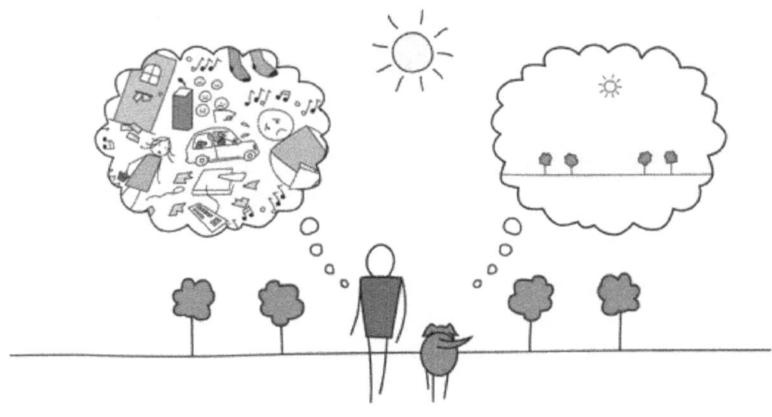

Mindfulness is the ability to accept every moment peacefully and nonjudgmentally. Being mindful means that you stay in the present moment without attaching any sort of judgments and labels to things you experience. When you are mindful, you accept things the way they are without letting them dampen your spirits, agitate you or weaken you emotionally.

Also, mindfulness improves your awareness of your emotions, which helps you manage them better. You become conscious of the different emotions and feelings you experience instantly and make sure they do not influence you negatively. Therefore, if you feel hurt because of losing a contest, you acknowledge that and combat it positively so that hurt doesn't dampen your motivation to work harder towards your goals.

To become mindful, start doing every task consciously. When you perform a task, bring every ounce of your awareness to it and do it with full attention. This improves your interest in it and helps you stay aware of every moment as it passes by.

Practice Deep Breathing

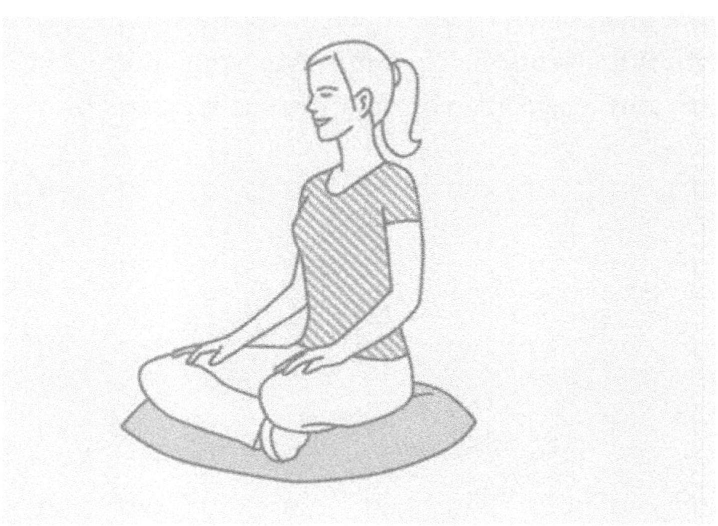

When you become anxious, your breath becomes shallow and rapid. This is perceived as a trigger of danger by your body and it releases cortisol, a stress hormone, in your bloodstream, which increases your stress levels and further exacerbates your stress and anxiety. A good way to combat this issue is to make a habit of breathing deeply.

Every day before beginning your routine chores, take 5 minutes to practice deep breathing. This clears your head, relaxes your nerves, reduces anxiety and trains you to breathe deeply.

To practice deep breathing, inhale to a count of 6 from your nose; hold that breath to another count of 6 and release it to a count of 6 or 7. Do it for 5 minutes and you will feel a beautiful sense of calmness inside you.

Practice this every 3 to 4 hours and after a few days, increase its frequency. Soon you will inculcate in yourself the habit of breathing calmly, which will only strengthen your confidence and the ability to think rationally.

Face Your Fears

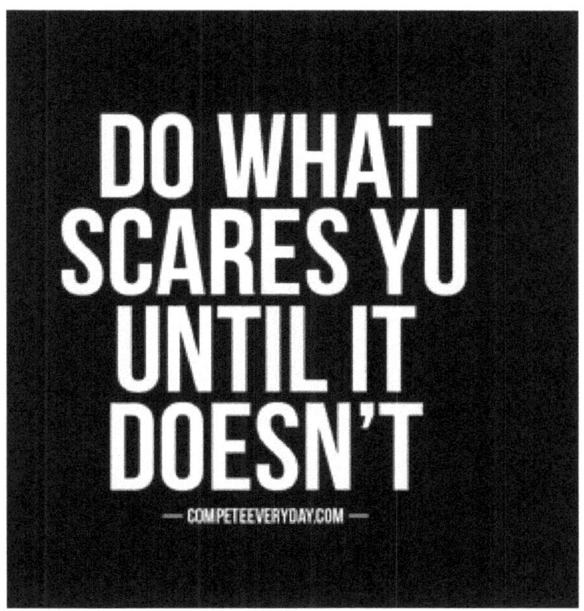

Often, anxiety and emotional weakness is rooted in avoiding your fears and not combatting them openly. When you keep avoiding things that intimidate you, you are indirectly telling yourself that you are incompetent to battle your obstacles and this only lowers your self-belief.

To break this vicious cycle, start facing your fears. Make a list of all your fears and try to slowly face them every day or week. For instance, if you are scared of quitting your job and pursuing your business, make a commitment to yourself to start the business you are passionate about as a part-time endeavor in the first week and work hard on it to earn a living from it. Make it a mission to do so in 3 to 4 months and as you move closer to your goal, slowly cut back on the hours of your day job.

Similarly, whatever your fears are, slowly encourage yourself to face them so you become emotionally stronger and resilient.

Set Bigger Challenges

Another ritual you need to bring in to your workout regimen is to set bigger challenges for yourself with each passing day. Therefore, if you can breathe deeply for 5 minutes, try to do it for 10 minutes. If you can control your anger for 15 minutes, try to do it for 30 minutes. If you have been able to start your business, now set a challenge to boost your sales by 20% the next month. As you slowly climb up the 'challenge' ladder, you inculcate in yourself the ability to try new things without losing your calm.

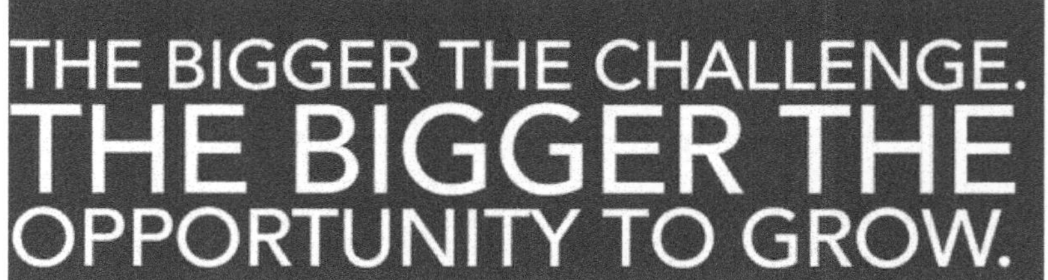

Work on these practices consistently and incorporate them into your life to build the emotional strength to take charge of your life.

Conclusion

I hope this book provided you with the value you were searching for. Employ the techniques in the book to have better control of your emotions and become empowered within and beyond.

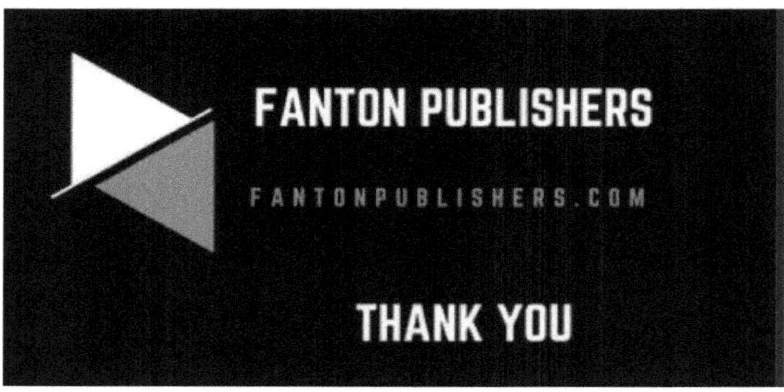

Do You Like My Book & Approach To Publishing?

If you like my writing and style and would love the ease of learning literally everything you can get your hands on from Fantonpublishers.com, I'd really need you to do me either of the following favors.

1: First, I'd Love It If You Leave a Review of This Book on Amazon.

2: Check Out My Emotional Mastery Books

Note: This list may not represent all my Keto diet books. You can check the full list by visiting my author page.

<u>Emotional Intelligence: The Mindfulness Guide To Mastering Your Emotions, Getting Ahead And Improving Your Life</u>

<u>Stress: The Psychology of Managing Pressure: Practical Strategies to turn Pressure into Positive Energy (5 Key Stress Techniques for Stress, Anxiety, and Depression Relief)</u>

<u>Failure Is Not The END: It Is An Emotional Gym: Complete Workout Plan On How To Build Your Emotional Muscle And Burning Down Anxiety To Become Emotionally Stronger, More Confident and Less Reactive</u>

[Subconscious Mind: Tame, Reprogram & Control Your Subconscious Mind To Transform Your Life](#)

[Body Language: Master Body Language: A Practical Guide to Understanding Nonverbal Communication and Improving Your Relationships](#)

[Shame and Guilt: Overcoming Shame and Guilt: Step By Step Guide On How to Overcome Shame and Guilt for Good](#)

[Anger Management: A Simple Guide on How to Deal with Anger](#)

Get updates when we publish any book that will help you master your emotions: http://bit.ly/2fantonpubpersonaldevl

To get a list of all my other books, please fantonwriters.com, my author central or let me send you the list by requesting them below: http://bit.ly/2fantonpubnewbooks

3: Grab Some Freebies On Your Way Out; Giving Is Receiving, Right?

I gave you a complimentary book at the start of the book. If you are still interested, grab it here.

[5 Pillar Life Transformation Checklist](#): http://bit.ly/2fantonfreebie

PSS: Let Me Also Help You Save Some Money!

If you are a heavy reader, have you considered subscribing to Kindle Unlimited? You can read this and millions of other books for just $9.99 a month)! You can check it out by searching for Kindle Unlimited on Amazon!